I Love to Draw & Paint!

Jennifer Lipsey

Sterling Publishing Co., Inc.
New York

My Very Favorite Art Book

D1304932

This book is dedicated
to the kids at Veritas

Editor
JOE RHATIGAN

Creative Director
CELIA NARANJO

Associate Art Director
SHANNON YOKELEY

Editorial Assistance
DELORES GOSNELL

Library of Congress Cataloging-in-Publication Data Available

10 9 8 7 6 5 4 3 2 1

First Edition

Published by Sterling Publishing Co., Inc.
387 Park Avenue South, New York, N.Y. 10016
This book is comprised of the following titles published by Lark Books,
A Division of Sterling Publishing Co., Inc.:
My Very Favorite Art Book : I Love to Draw! © 2005 by Jennifer Lipsey
My Very Favorite Art Book : I Love to Paint! © 2005 by Jennifer Lipsey

Distributed in Canada by Sterling Publishing,
c/o Canadian Manda Group, 165 Dufferin Street
Toronto, Ontario, Canada M6K 3H6

Distributed in the United Kingdom by GMC Distribution Services,
Castle Place, 166 High Street, Lewes, East Sussex, England BN7 1XU

Distributed in Australia by Capricorn Link (Australia) Pty Ltd.
P.O. Box 704, Windsor, NSW 2756 Australia

The written instructions, photographs, designs, patterns, and projects in this volume are intended for the personal use of the reader and may be reproduced for that purpose only. Any other use, especially commercial use, is forbidden under law without written permission of the copyright holder.

Every effort has been made to ensure that all the information in this book is accurate. However, due to differing conditions, tools, and individual skills, the publisher cannot be responsible for any injuries, losses, and other damages that may result from the use of the information in this book.

Manufactured in China
All rights reserved

Sterling ISBN-13: 978-1-4027-4543-0
       ISBN-10: 1-4027-4543-5

For information about custom editions, special sales, premium and corporate purchases, please contact Sterling Special Sales Department at 800-805-5489 or specialsales@sterlingpub.com.

CONTENTS

Art is Awesome!

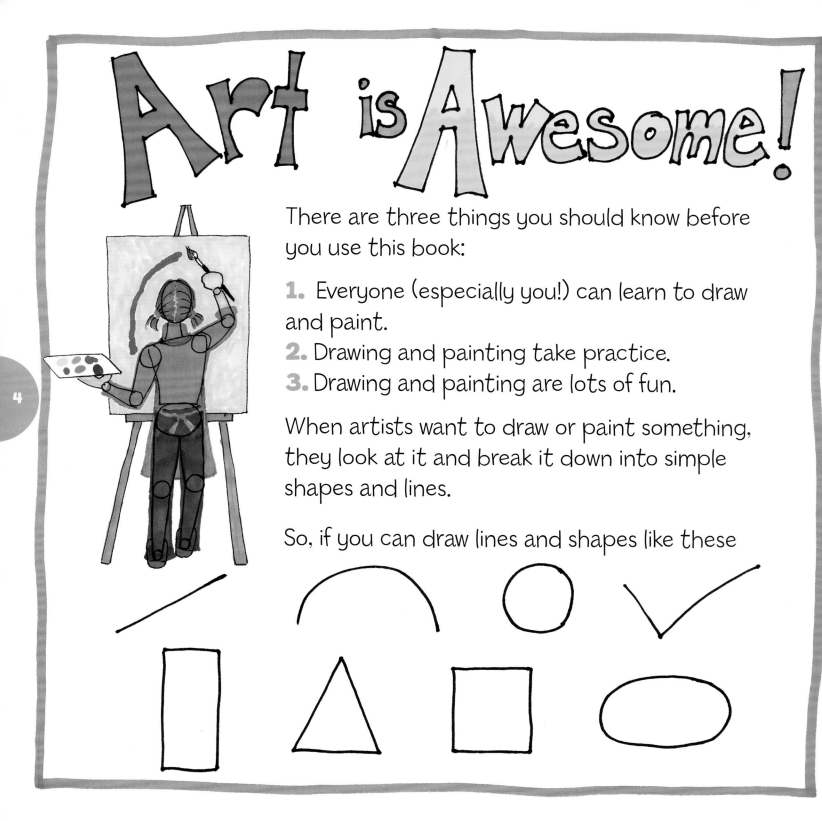

There are three things you should know before you use this book:

1. Everyone (especially you!) can learn to draw and paint.
2. Drawing and painting take practice.
3. Drawing and painting are lots of fun.

When artists want to draw or paint something, they look at it and break it down into simple shapes and lines.

So, if you can draw lines and shapes like these

then, with some practice, you will be able to put them together in fun and different ways to draw things like these:

Let's start now with drawing. Then we'll move on to painting!

Drawing is something you can do almost anywhere.

You can draw in your or in a

or at a  or even up a .

All you need to get started is a

and some

The drawings in this book are colored in with

but you can also use

or

The pages on the left side of this book show lots of cool instructions.

Each new step is shown in PINK. The steps already finished are in **BLACK**. Like this:

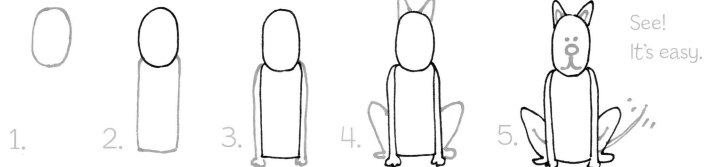

1. 2. 3. 4. 5.

See! It's easy.

Use a pencil to draw your objects. Draw lightly so it will be easy to erase any extra lines. Then, add color if you want.

The pages on the right side of the book show fun ways to use what you've learned.

Underwater

FISH

1.　　　　2.　　　　3.　　　　4.　　　　5.　　　　Add some stripes.

BLOWFISH

1.　　　　2.　　　　3.

UNDERWATER PLANT

1.　　　　2.　　　　3.

CLOWN FISH

1.　　　　2.　　　　3.　　　　4.

SHARK

  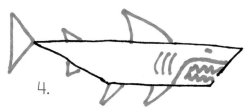

1.　　　　2.　　　　3.　　　　4.

Erase the extra lines.

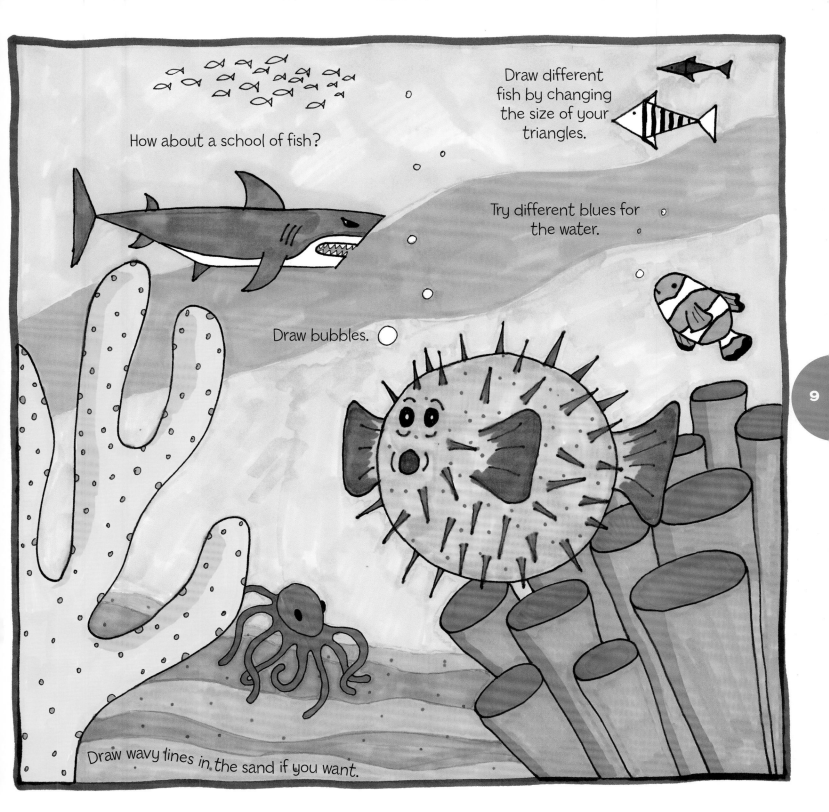

How about a school of fish?

Draw different fish by changing the size of your triangles.

Try different blues for the water.

Draw bubbles.

Draw wavy lines in the sand if you want.

9

Bugs

CATERPILLAR

1.

2.

3.

BUTTERFLY

1.

2.

3.

10

OVERLAPPING GRASS

SNAIL

1.

2.

3.

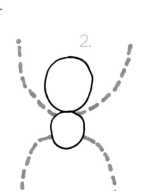

LADYBUG

1.   1.

2.   2.

SPIDER

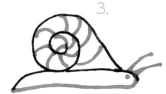

1.

2.

3.

Use different colors and patterns for your butterflies.

How hungry is your caterpillar?

Trees

PALM TREE

1.

2.

3.

4.

OAK TREE

1.

2.

3.

PINE TREE

1.

2.

3. Erase extra lines. Draw branches.

WILLOW TREE

1.

2.

3.

Flowers

DAISY

1.

2.

3.

4.

5.

14

TULIP

1.

2.

3.

4.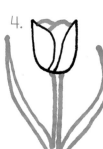

ROSE

1.

2.

3.

4.

5.

FLOWER IN A VASE

SUNFLOWER

Turn your paper as you draw the petals.

1.

2.

3.

Things drawn small at the top of your page look far away.

Want to draw a barn? See page 23.

Things drawn big at the bottom of the page look close up.

Sweets

ICE CREAM CONE

 1.

 2.

 3.

 4.

Don't forget the cherry on top!

Add more scoops!

HARD CANDY

 1.

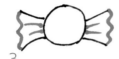 2.

 3.

ICE POP

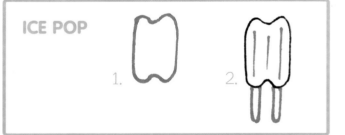

1.   2.

CUPCAKE

 1.

 2.

 3.

 4.

Add frosting and sprinkles. Yum!

BIRTHDAY CAKE

 1.

2.   3.

Blow out the candles.

CHOCOLATE CHIP COOKIE

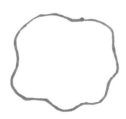

Winter

SNOWMAN

1.

2.

The first snowball overlaps the second one.

3.

4.

Now decorate!
Don't forget the hat.

18

CHRISTMAS TREE

1.

It's good if your branches look different.

2.

Don't forget the trunk.

3.

Draw one line under the trunk and another one behind the trunk for snow. Add more branches, and decorate!

HOLLY BERRIES

1.

2.

3.

CANDY CANE

SNOWFLAKE

1.

2.

3.

4.

Try different
snowflake designs.

How about a snowlady?

Turn to page 26 to
draw cool boxes.

19

Mountains

HILLS

1.

2.

3.

MOUNTAINS

1.

2.

3.

Add as many
mountains as you want.

SNOWY MOUNTAINS

1.

2.

3.

VOLCANO

1.

2.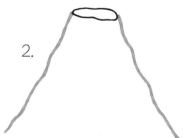

3.

Draw rocks
and lava.

Buildings

HOUSE

1.

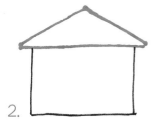

2.

3.

Add the windows.

4.

CHURCH

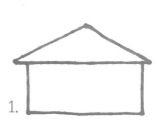

1.

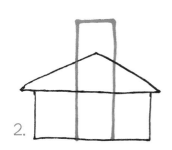

2.

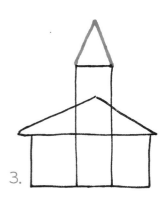

3.

4.

Erase extra lines and
add a door and windows.

CASTLE

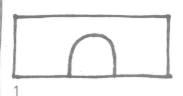

1.

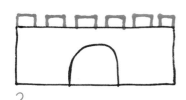

2.

3.

4.

22

BARN

1.

2.

3.

4. Add a silo, doors, and a window.

What animals live on your farm?

23

The Big City

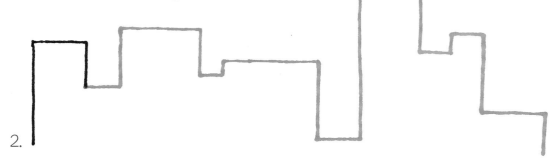

1.

Start like this.

2.

Now keep drawing without lifting your pencil from the paper.

Now add lots of details, such as windows, chimneys, domes, towers, and steeples.

3.

Now try drawing another city line that overlaps the first one. Erase extra lines.

4.

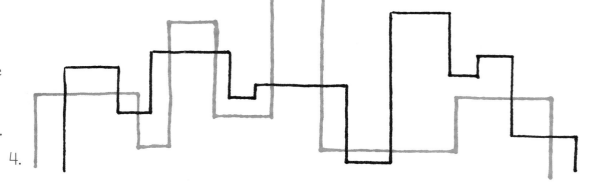

MORNING

Use more than one sky color.

Color around the sun to leave it white.

DAY

Leave white in the sky to show clouds.

NIGHT

When coloring the sky, leave tiny bits of white for the stars.

To make a whole building look lit up, color the yellow in first, and then draw thick black lines on top for windows.

3-D Objects

CUBE

1.
Draw a square with a dot in the middle.

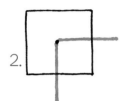
2.
Draw another square on top of the first one, starting from the dot.

3.

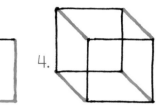
4.
Connect the four corners.

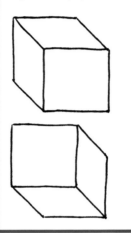
Erase lines to make the cube look solid.

CONE

1.
Draw an oval.

2.
Center a dot above the oval.

3.
Connect the dot to the sides of the oval.

CYLINDER

1.
Draw an oval.

2.
Draw another above the first.

3.
Connect the sides with straight lines.

3-D ROAD

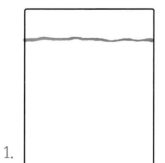
1.
Draw a line toward the top of your paper.

2.
Put a dot on the line.

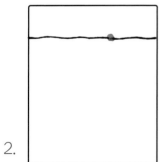
3.
Draw a triangle down from the line.

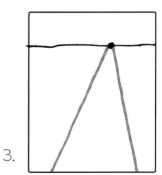
4.
Draw a dotted line down the middle.

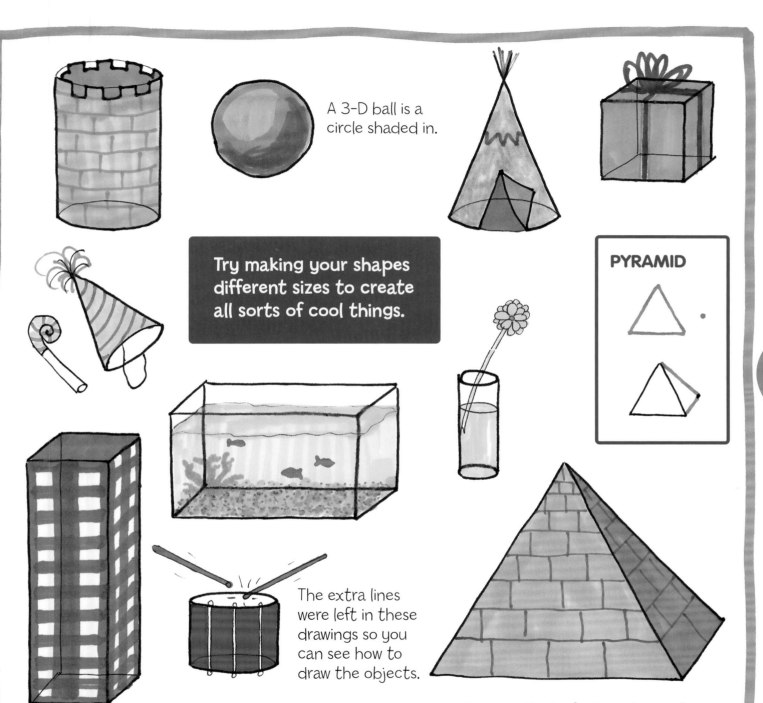

A 3-D ball is a circle shaded in.

PYRAMID

Try making your shapes different sizes to create all sorts of cool things.

The extra lines were left in these drawings so you can see how to draw the objects.

Can you think of other objects? How about a TV? A soda can?

Dogs & Cats

STANDING CAT

1.

2.

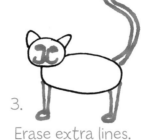

3.

Erase extra lines.

NAPPING CAT

STRETCHING CAT

1.

2.

3.

Erase the extra line in the head.

4.

BIG DOG

1.

2.

3.

What color will your dog be?

SITTING DOG

1.

2.

3.

4.

LITTLE DOG

1.

2.

3.

Erase extra neck lines.
Add details and shaggy hair.

Try floppy ears.

Does your kitty like to look out the window?

Go to page 12 for more trees.

Try pointy ears.

Draw the hair sticking up on a stretching cat to make it a scared cat.

Check out the people on page 38!

Birds

PENGUIN

1.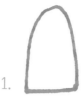
2.
3.
4.

TROPICAL FLOWER

1.
2.
3.

FLAMINGO

1.
2.
3.
4.

TOUCAN

1.
2.
3.
4.

CHICK

Add tiny lines to make it fuzzy.

HEN

1.
2.
3.

BARN OWL

1.
2.
3.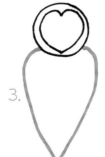
4.

Make up your own silly bird.

31

Animals

PIG

1.

2.

3.

FROG

1.

2.

3.

MONKEY

1.

Draw the arm and leg joints.

2.

See the people on page 38 for help.

Connect the arms and legs.

3.

Erase extra lines.

Add details.

32

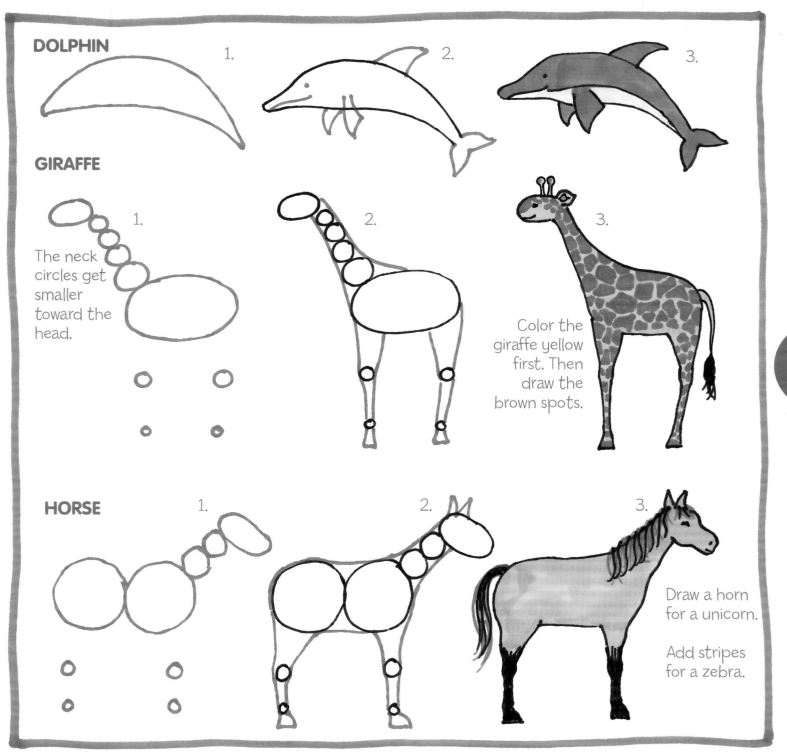

DOLPHIN

1.

2.

3.

GIRAFFE

The neck circles get smaller toward the head.

1.

2.

3.

Color the giraffe yellow first. Then draw the brown spots.

33

HORSE

1.

2.

3.

Draw a horn for a unicorn.

Add stripes for a zebra.

Dinosaurs

APATOSAURUS

1.

2.

Add on six more circles and an oval for the head.

Nobody knows what colors and patterns dinosaurs were. So use your imagination when you color them.

3.

Draw a line around the body that touches all the circles. Draw the legs.

4. Erase the circles and the lines inside the legs closest to you. Add eyes and a mouth.

TRICERATOPS

1.

Leave a small space between the head and the body.

2.

3.

Draw the horns and mouth.

Erase extra lines. Add more details.

4.

STEGOSAURUS

Want to draw hills and volcanoes? See page 20.

Learn to draw palm trees. See page 12.

TYRANNOSAURUS REX

Faces

1.

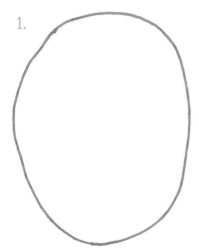

Draw an upside down egg shape.

2.

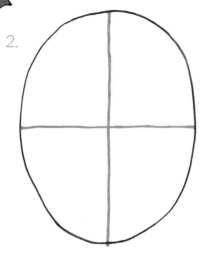

Divide it in half both ways.

3.

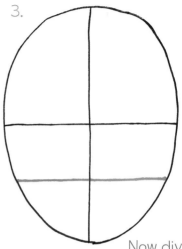

Now divide the bottom half.

4.

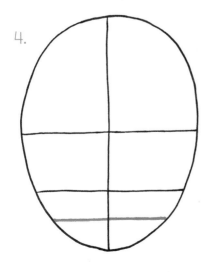

Do it again.

5.

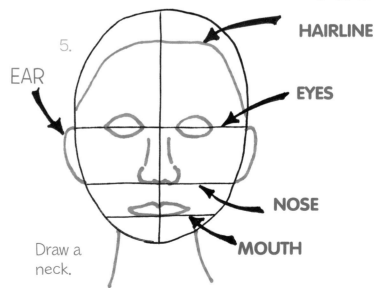

HAIRLINE

EAR

EYES

NOSE

MOUTH

Draw a neck.

Now you know where all the parts of the face belong.

Erase the lines after you draw all the features.

Try different skin colors.

Don't forget eyelids and eyebrows.

Draw different hairstyles and colors.

How about a hat?

MAD

HAPPY

SURPRISED

SCARED

SILLY

SAD

NAUGHTY

Look closely in the mirror and practice drawing your face. This is called a self-portrait.

People

THE BODY

1.

Draw an oval head. Add the neck.

2.

Draw the torso.

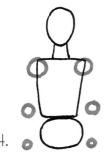

3.

Draw an oval for the hips.

Draw large circles that overlap the torso for shoulders.

4.

Draw medium circles for the elbows and small circles for the wrists.

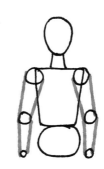

5.

Connect the circles to make arms. See how the arms get skinnier at the wrists?

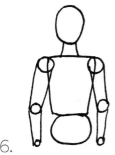

6.

Draw large circles for the knees and medium circles for the ankles.

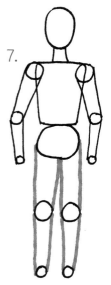

7.

Connect the circles to make legs.

8.

Draw simple hands and feet.

Don't make them too small.

DIVER

BALLERINA

QUEEN

You can create lots of different kinds of people with the simple body you just learned to draw. Always draw the body first, and then add the clothes. Erase lines you don't want to show or just color over them.

KING

Draw wide body shapes for thick people.

BASKETBALL PLAYER

Draw narrow body shapes for thin people.

Make the body shape longer and the arm and leg circles farther apart for a tall person.

39

More People

SCIENTIST

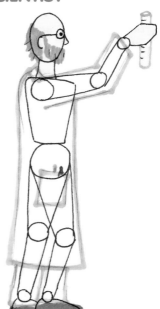

SOCCER BALL

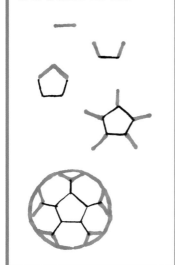

YOUNG SOCCER PLAYER

Make the body shapes smaller and closer together for a little person.

MUSICIAN

Try tilting the head.

PIRATE

Make the shapes bigger and farther apart for a big person.

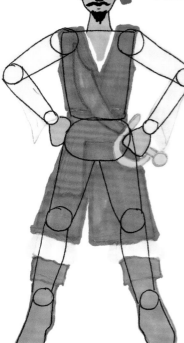

PRINCESS

FAIRY

Draw the wings after you draw the body.

WIZARD

Color the beard first, and then color the robe around the beard.

YOUNG ARTIST

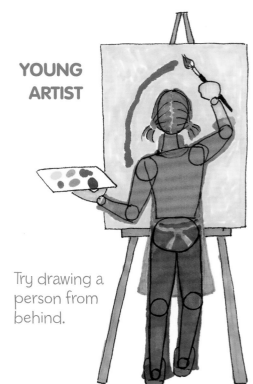

Try drawing a person from behind.

Medieval Fantasy

TROLL

1.

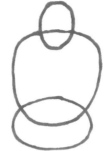

Draw the head, torso, and hips.

2.

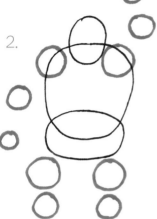

Draw the arm and leg joints.

3.

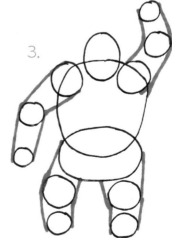

Connect the circles to make arms and legs.

4.

Erase extra lines and add feet, hands, and a face. Don't forget the club!

DRAGON

1.

2.

Outline the body circles and draw legs.

3.

Add wings, teeth, spikes, scales, and horns.

See page 22 for castles.

See page 39 for more Medieval people.

KNIGHT

1.

2. Add the arm and leg joints.

3. Connect the joints. Add weapons and armor.

Cars & Trucks

SEMI-TRUCK

1.
2.
3.

PICKUP TRUCK

1.
2.

3.
4.

Add windows, bumpers, and other details.

SPORTS CAR

1.
2.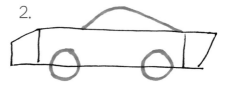

3.
4.

Erase the extra lines, and add details.

BEETLE

1.
2.
3.
4.

44

Draw a city.
See page 24.

Stop

Draw some
parking
meters.

Wheels

MOUNTAIN BIKE

1.

2.

3. Add a seat and handlebars.

4.

Draw the wheels.

5.

Add pedals, spokes, and tires.

MOTORCYCLE

1. Draw the tire and wheel.

2. Draw the fender, seat, and gas tank.

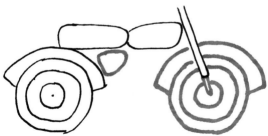

3. Add the front wheel and fender.

4. Add handlebars, headlight, and exhaust pipe.

SCOOTER

1.

2.

3. Draw the tires.

4. Erase extra lines. Add the seat, handlebars, and details.

See page 38 for people.

Draw skakeboards!

Paint is Great!

Painting is fun, and anyone can do it!

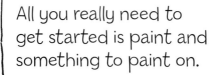

All you really need to get started is paint and something to paint on.

A paintbrush is handy, too, if you don't always want to paint with your fingers.

Your paintings can look like something real...

But they don't have to.

Both are awesome!

This book will show you lots of cool ways to paint. You will see how to paint with sponges, toothpicks, rollers, and even straws! There are loads of projects and examples so you will never run out of ideas.

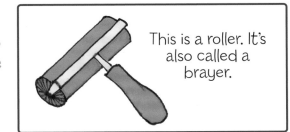

This is a roller. It's also called a brayer.

Painting goes all the way back to caveman (and woman) times. Even then, cave dwellers had to gather their supplies before they started painting, and so will you.

Supplies

Paint Brushes

come in many shapes and sizes.

Small brushes are good for painting small shapes and details.

Take good care of your brushes by washing them out with warm water when you're done.

Large, flat brushes are good for big shapes and spaces. Practice different brush strokes with your paintbrushes.

Paint

In this book, we will work with lots of different art supplies.

These are the three main paints we will be working with:

Paint

Watercolors

Crayons

Tempera paints and poster paints are the same thing.

They come in bottles or jars.

The paint is ready to use as soon as you open it. You can use acrylic paints, too.

Watercolor paints usually come in a case like this one.

You have to wet this paint first to make it work.

Yes, you can paint with crayons!

Keep your broken crayons handy. You'll see why.

a Palette

This is the thing that holds your paint. It's easier to mix colors if you use one.

A palette doesn't have to be fancy.

It can be something you can use over and over again, such as a dinner plate or an old cookie sheet.

Or, it can be something you throw out when you're done, such as a foam plate.

Here's how to make your own palette.

1. Staple 10 pieces of waxed paper to a piece of cardboard.

2. The waxed paper is your palette. Simply rip off the top sheet when you're done painting. The next sheet is clean!

Paper

You can paint on most any kind of paper.

Some projects in this book call for thin paper, while others work better on thick paper.

Here are ideas for thin and thick papers you might find for free:

newspaper
junk mail
wrapping paper
computer paper
coffee filters

Thin

cereal boxes   manila folders
construction paper   old greeting cards
cardboard

Thick

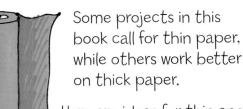

Set Up

1. Put on some old clothes or an apron.

2. Lay out some newspaper, an old sheet, or a shower curtain to protect the table or floor you are going to be working on.

3. Get out your supplies and this book. Have fun!

Clean Up

1. Lay your paintings someplace safe to dry.

2. Throw out the used water. Wash your brushes and tools.

3. Put everything away.

4. Throw out the newspaper or fold up the sheet.

HINT: Adults will let you paint more often if you keep your art things clean and neat. Guaranteed!

52

Make an Art Kit

Use a cardboard box or a plastic bin to hold all of your art supplies. This will be your Art Kit.

With an Art Kit, you will always know where your supplies are, and it makes set up and clean up much easier.

Here are supplies to include in your Art Kit:

- Paint
- Pencils
- Eraser
- Markers
- Crayons
- Brushes
- Palette
- Paper
- Glue
- Water container
- Rollers and cans
- Sponges
- Old toothbrush
- Scissors
- Paper towels
- Cardboard tubes
- Newspaper

Color

The only colors you really need are red, yellow, blue, black, and white. With some color math you can mix any color you want.

Here's how:

Red + Blue = Purple

Yellow + Red = Orange

Blue + Yellow = Green

What happens when you add white or black to a color?

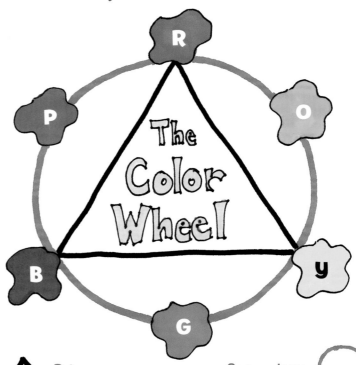

The Color Wheel

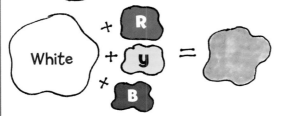

Mix SKIN Colors

White + R + y + B =

Start with white. Add a little of the three primary colors until you get the skin color you want.

△ Primary Colors

These make other colors:
Red
Yellow
Blue

○ Secondary Colors

These are made from primary colors:
Purple
Orange
Green

Let's Paint!

Finger-paint Fun!

1.

Put small puddles of paint on your palette.

If you want, draw a picture in pencil first.

2.

Now touch your finger to a paint puddle. Use your finger like a paintbrush.

Don't forget to wipe your finger on a paper towel when you want to change colors.

Fill up the whole page.

Try using different fingers. What happens if you use two or three fingers at once?

3.

Supplies

* Tempera paint
* Palette
* Paper
* Paper towels
* Your fingers!

Finger-paint an underwater scene.

Why not try a prehistoric scene?

Use fingerprints for the sun and the coconuts.

Wild Watercolors!

1. Lightly draw a shape with your pencil.

2. Carefully paint the whole shape with clear water.

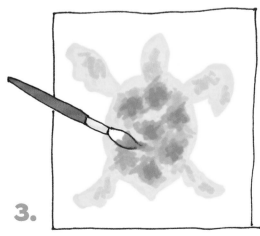

3.

Use the other brush to put watercolor on the wet shape.

The paint will stay inside the shape!

Paint until the shape is filled with color.

Supplies

* Pencil
* Thick paper
* 2 paintbrushes
* Water cup
* Watercolor paint

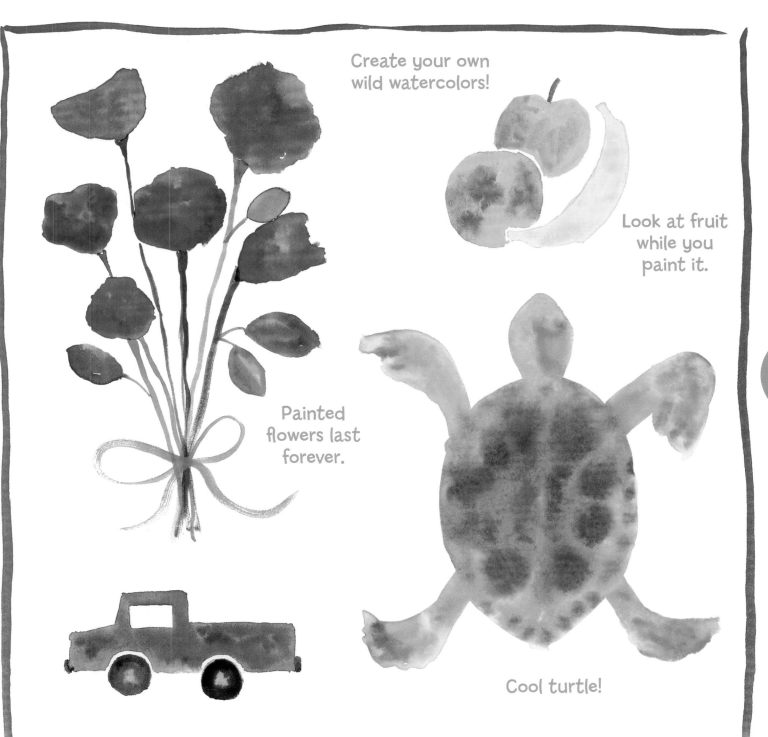

Create your own wild watercolors!

Look at fruit while you paint it.

Painted flowers last forever.

Cool turtle!

Blob & Blot

1. Fold a piece of paper in half.

2. Unfold the paper, and put a few drops of paint near the middle.

3. Fold the paper in half again. Press and rub all over the paper.

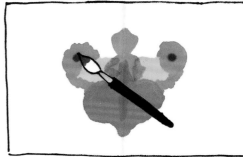

4. Open the paper again. If you like what you see, let it dry.

Or, you can add more paint and fold it again. Let it dry.

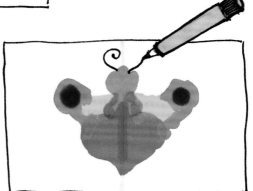

Now look closely at your paint blot. Do you see something in it?

Use markers to add details.

5.

Supplies
* Paper
* Tempera paint
* Palette
* Paintbrush
* Water cup
* Markers

Use markers to add details to
your paint blot. What do you
see in your paint blots?

A butterfly?

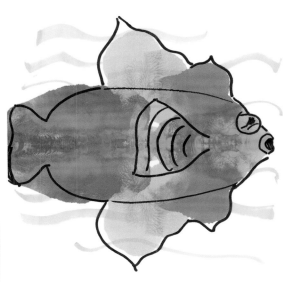

A monster?

Tape Painting

1.
Make a picture with pieces of masking tape.

2.
Paint over your tape picture. Let your colors mix together if you want.

3.
After the painting dries, peel off the tape. Awesome!

Try this!
Make a tape picture on top of a finished painting. Paint it again, and remove the tape. Wow!

Supplies
* Paper
* Masking tape
* Watercolor paint
* Paintbrush
* Water cup

Try a flower!

Scratch Magic!

1. Draw a picture with a pencil very lightly.

2. Firmly scratch over the pencil lines with a pushpin or other tool. Erase the pencil lines.

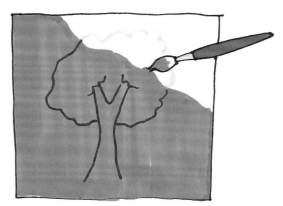

3. Paint over your whole picture. Your drawing appears like magic!

Supplies
* Thick paper
* Pencil
* Pushpin, nail, or large paperclip
* Eraser
* Watercolor paint
* Paintbrush
* Water cup

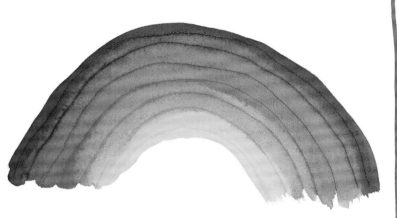

Try different colors!

You can use a tissue to blot parts you want to make lighter.

Watch out for that shark!

Rock & Roll

1.

Paint your roller.

Roll on moist paper towels to clean the roller.

2.

Roll it onto the paper.

3.

See what happens when you paint a shape on the roller.

Cool!

Supplies
* Roller
* Tempera paint
* Palette
* Paintbrush
* Water cup
* Paper

Roll a giant.

Use your roller to create the body. Paint small trees or houses to show how big he (or she!) is.

Use a sponge for the giant's hair and for the treetops.

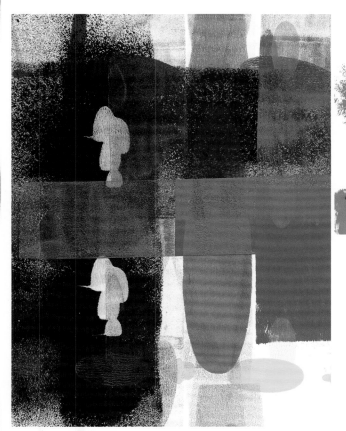

Roller designs also make a nice background for drawings.

Roll a cool design by overlapping different colors.

Sponge Blob!

Sponges come in many sizes, shapes, and colors. Have a parent cut a big sponge into small, easy-to-hold pieces.

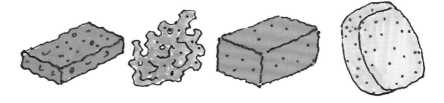

1.

Brush or squirt colors you want to use onto your palette.

2.

Dip the sponge in some paint. See what happens when you twist, blot, and sweep the sponge on the paper.

> **Clean your sponges by dipping them in water and squeezing all the paint out.**

Try this!

Wet your paper with water and a clean sponge. Then, sponge paint on the wet paper. So cool!

or

Use scissors to cut shapes from a thin sponge. Use them like stamps.

Supplies

* Sponges
* Scissors
* Tempera paint
* Palette
* Paintbrush
* Water cup
* Paper

SPONGE

You can buy sponges that are already cut into shapes.

Cut out shapes to make a picture.

Use the corners, edges, and sides of the sponge.

Try twists, dots, and lines on wet paper.

Dot to Dot

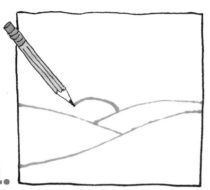

1. Lightly draw a simple picture with a pencil.

2. Gently press the eraser on your paint pad.

3. Fill up one section of your picture with dots.

> When you're ready to change colors, clean the eraser by blotting it on a moist paper towel.

4. Fill in other sections of your picture with dots.

Make a Paint Pad

1. Fold a wet paper towel to fit on top of a plate.

2. Brush paint on the paper towel.

Make a paint pad for each color you use.

Supplies
* Paper
* Pencil with a new eraser
* Paper towels
* Water
* Plate
* Tempera paint

Trace something square or round.

Make dot frames for your favorite paintings.

Mix your colors!

How about a dotted sunrise?

Try some flowers.

Use a brush to paint the stems.

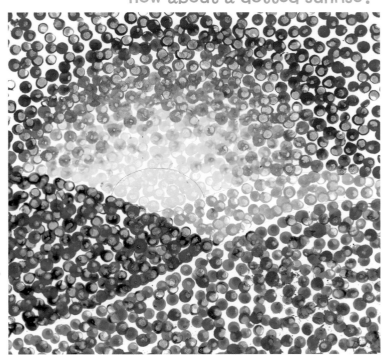

Finger Printing

Did you know you can paint lots of different shapes with your fingers? Check it out!

Thumb   Index finger   Middle finger   Ring finger   Side of the pinky

Pinky   Ring   Middle   Index   Thumb

Practice these prints by pressing the underside of your fingertips onto the paint pad. Then press your finger onto the paper.

Soft ring finger: Press gently to make a small print.

Hard ring finger: Press harder to make a big print.

Try this!

Index

Thumb

Thumb sideways

1.

Pinky side

Pinky side

2.

Pinky side

Ring soft

Ring hard

3.

Supplies

* Paint pads (see page 68)
* Tempera paint
* Paper
* Your fingers

Can you figure out which fingers were used to make these pictures?

Touchdown!

Where's my suntan lotion?

Wet Wax!

1. Draw a picture with your pencil.

2. Color it in with crayons. Press down hard, and leave a little white paper showing.

3. Paint the whole picture with black paint. Looks awesome, doesn't it?

Try This!

1. Use a black crayon to draw your picture. Don't forget to press down hard.

2. Color your picture in with crayons. Leave some white showing. Then, paint it with bright watercolors.

Supplies
* Pencil
* Paper
* Crayons
* Watercolor paints
* Paintbrush
* Water cup

72

Look in the mirror and try drawing a self-portrait.

How about a toucan in the jungle?

Super Stencil!

1.
Fold your piece of paper in half. Draw half of a shape on it.

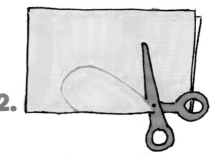

2.
Keep the paper folded and cut out the shape. Open up the two pieces.

3.
Dip your paintbrush in some paint. Brush most of the paint onto a paper towel.

4.
Hold the stencil on a new piece of paper. Start on the stencil and brush toward the middle.

5.
Try using the other piece you cut out in step 2. Paint away from the shape.

Supplies
* Thick paper
* Pencil
* Scissors
* Tempera paint
* Palette
* Flat paintbrush
* Water cup
* Paper towels

Here you can see both pieces.

Try overlapping shapes and colors.

Make a mountain stencil.

Soggy Art!

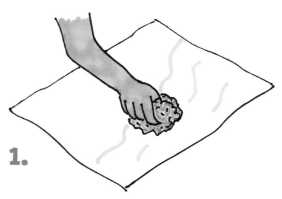

1. Use a wet sponge to moisten the paper all over.

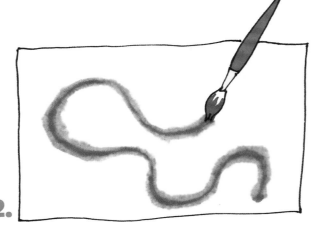

2. Paint on the wet paper. Watch the colors spread out and blend together.

> Don't forget to wash your paintbrush before you change colors.

Try this!

1. Wet the paper. Paint a sky and leave the ground white.

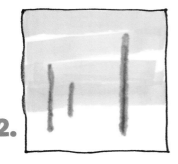

2. While the paper is still wet, paint lines where you want trees.

3. Paint tall squiggly triangle shapes on the lines.

Supplies

* Thick paper
* Wet sponge
* Tempera paint
* Palette
* Paintbrush
* Water cup

Paint a squiggly line all over your wet paper. Fill in the leftover spaces with a different color.

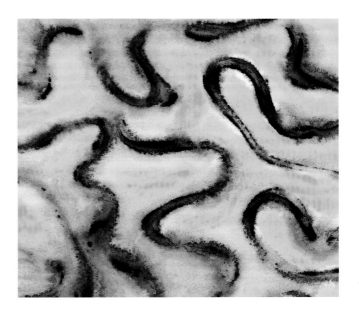

Try using lots of different colors on the wet paper.

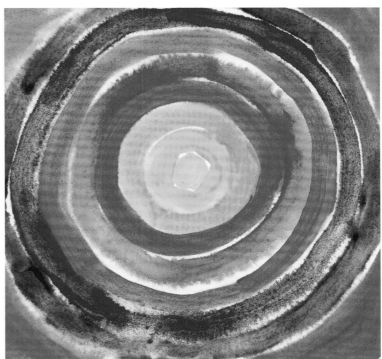

Straw Painting

1. Put a small puddle of watercolor or watered down tempera paint on your paper.

2. Aim the straw where you want the paint to move and BLOW!

Try blowing with two straws at the same time.

Try this!

1. Paint a sunset with black land. Let it dry.

A sunset silhouette!

2. Blow black trees up from the land.

Supplies

* Paper
* Paintbrush
* Watercolor paint or watered-down tempera paint
* Water cup
* Straws

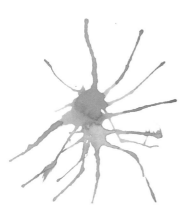

Try mixing up
your colors.

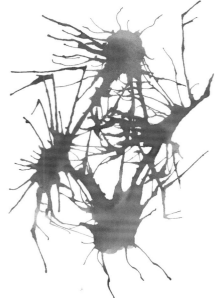

On a Roll!

1. Squirt a thin line of glue around your tube.

2. Push the string into the glue around the tube. Don't overlap it.

Make sure there aren't any loose spots where the string isn't glued. Let it dry.

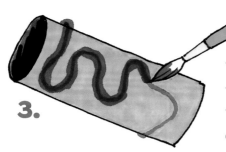

3. When the glue is dry, paint the string. Now roll it across the paper to see the string design.

Try this!

Cut out small cardboard or foam shapes and glue them to a tube.

Paint the shapes and roll the tube to see the pattern. Wow!

Supplies
* Cardboard tubes
* Glue
* String
* Tempera paint
* Paintbrush
* Palette
* Water cup
* Paper
* Cardboard
* Scissors

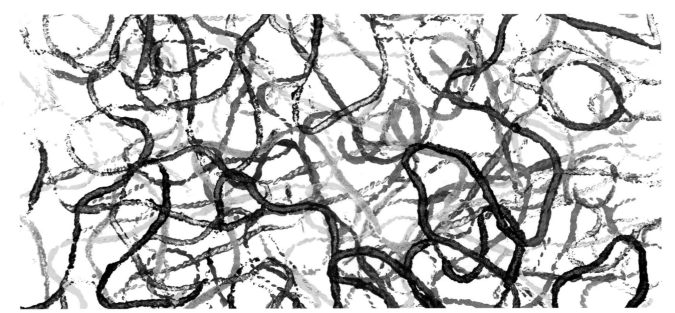

Try different colors on the same string.

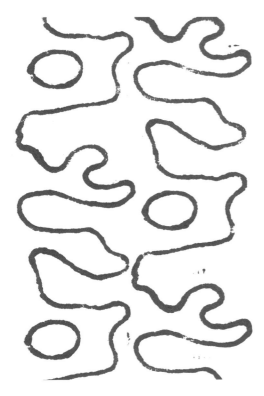

Make different color prints from the same tube.

All Cracked Up!

1.

Draw a picture with a pencil.

2.

Color it in with crayons. Use bright colors and press hard. Color in all the white parts.

3.

Crumple up your picture! Smooth it out and crumple it again.

4.

Smooth out the paper. Paint over it with a dark color.

5.

Gently rinse the paint off. Stop when there's only paint left in the cracks. Let it dry.

Supplies
* Pencil
* Paper
* Crayons
* Tempera paint
* Paintbrush
* Palette
* Water cup
* Sink

Draw a flamingo!

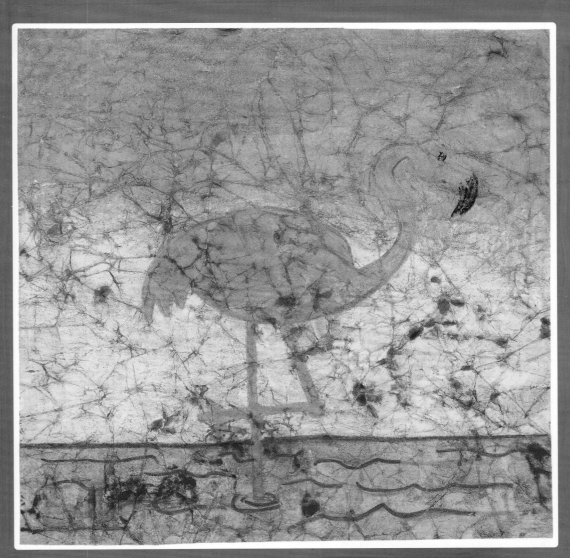

If you need to flatten your painting more, put it between two sheets of paper and have a parent iron it on low heat.

Scratch It!

1. Color your paper all over with bright colors. Press hard and cover all the white parts of your paper.

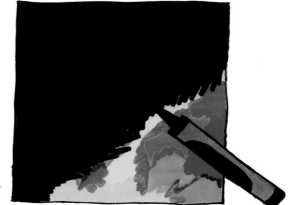

2. Color your paper over with the black crayon. Press hard and cover all the colors.

3. Use the nail, toothpick, or even your fingernail to scratch your picture.

Awesome!

Supplies
* Crayons
* Paper
* Nail, toothpick, paperclip, or something you can scratch with

You can "erase" a mistake by coloring over it with a black crayon.

Play & Spray!

How to spray paint:

1. Dip the toothbrush in a small paint puddle.

2. Hold the brush down over the paper.

Pull the bristles toward you with your finger.

The paint will spray away from you.

Re-dip when you start to run out of spray.

Clean the toothbrush between colors by swishing it in water. Dry it on a paper towel.

Now, for even more FUN!

1. Find flat things in and around your home. You can also cut out paper shapes. Place them on your paper.

2. Spray paint on top of the objects. Remove the objects after the paint dries. Cool!

Supplies

* Tempera paint
* Palette
* Old toothbrush
* Water cup
* Paper
* Flat objects

Make your initials with string.

Paint the paper first, and after it's dry, spray something over it.

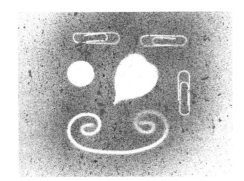

Try different designs.

Make a snowman!

Texture Treasures

Touch different things you see around you. The bottom of your shoe, a wall, screens, wood—these things feel different because they have different surface textures.

Crayon rubbings are pictures of each texture.

1. Find a texture and hold the paper on top of it. Rub the side of an unwrapped crayon across the paper.

2.

Find more textures, and make more rubbings on the same paper.

Try this!

See what happens when you paint with watercolors on top of your textured pictures.

It's cool!

Supplies

* Crayons
* Thin paper
* Textured objects
* Watercolor paint
* Paintbrush
* Water cup

Try lots of colors on one texture.

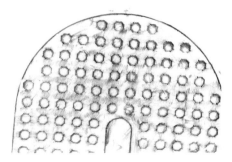

Can you guess what this is?

Paint it!

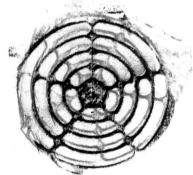

Textures are
everywhere!

Try different colors. Let the textures overlap.

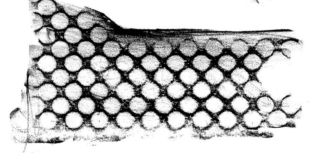

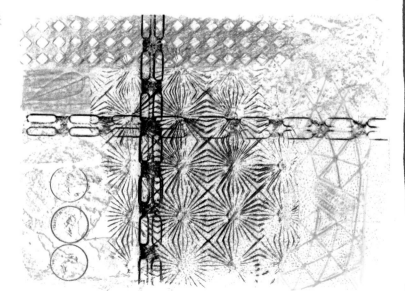

String's the Thing!

1.

Cut a piece of string or yarn about as long as your arm. Drop one end into a can of paint.

> Use a different piece of string for each color.

2.

Slowly pull the string out, and remove extra paint by squeezing it between a brush and the inside of the can.

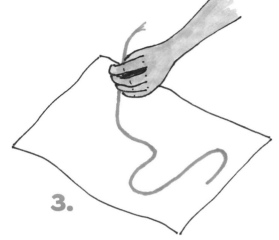

3.

Put the wet string on the paper. Drag it up, down, and all around. Use a new string and can for each color.

Try this!

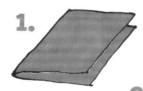

1.

Fold a piece of paper.

2.

Unfold it and place a painted string on one side. Hold onto one end of the string.

3.

Fold the paper, and hold it closed while you wiggle the string out. Open the paper. Wow!

Supplies
* String or yarn
* Scissors
* Tempera paint
* Cans
* Paintbrush
* Paper

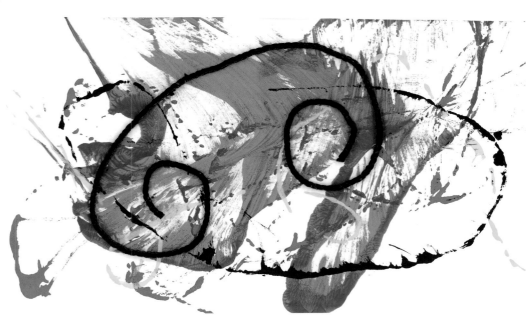

You can even glue your dried, painted string to the painting.

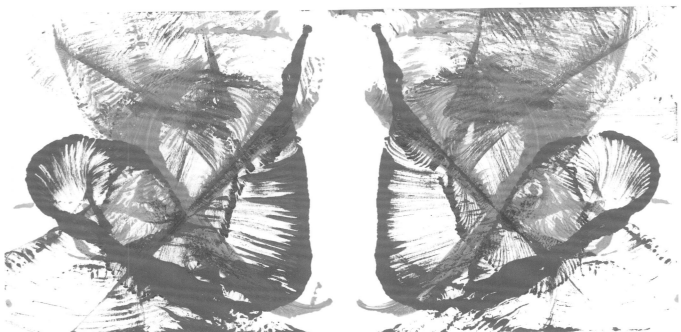

This design was done with a folded piece of paper.

Index

Acknowledgements

I would like to thank God and all the great people in my life who have shared the value of beauty, creativity, and hard work with me. I am very grateful to my art teachers from elementary school to graduate school—you have made all the difference, and I am honored to have become a part of this important legacy.

Big thanks to Joe, my editor, for believing in the importance of this series and taking a chance on an abstract painter writing and illustrating children's books.

Thanks to my wonderful group of friends and family who have been so supportive and understanding all the times I couldn't hang out because of The Books. Extra big thanks to my husband, Martin, for so much love, trips to the art store, reading all the Harry Potter books to me while I worked, and the delicious sweet tea and home-cooked meals delivered to the studio.
I love you.

Special thanks to my young art students at Veritas who have been such an inspiration and have kid-tested nearly all the projects in this book.
You're the greatest!

About the Author

Jennifer Lipsey is an accomplished artist and art teacher who has received numerous awards, scholarships, and grants. She lives in North Carolina.